OUR WILDLIFE WORLD

GIRAFFES

Merebeth Switzer

Grolier

FACTS IN BRIEF

Classification of the giraffe
    Class: *Mammalia* (mammals)
    Order: *Artiodactyla* (cloven-hoofed mammals)
    Family: *Giraffidae*
    Genus: *Giraffa*
    Species: *Giraffa camelopardalis.* Nine subspecies.

Distribution. Africa, south of the Sahara.

Habitat. Open woodlands and tree-dotted grasslands.

Distinctive physical characteristics. Extremely long neck; long, thin legs with front ones longer than hind; short horns covered with skin and hair; mottled orange-brown and white-cream coat.

Diet. Leaves and twigs, especially of acacia, mimosa and wild apricot.

Habits. Band together in loose groups; most active in early morning and evening.

This series is approved and recommended by the Federation of Ontario Naturalists.

Canadian Cataloguing in Publication Data

Switzer, Merebeth
  Giraffes

(Nature's children)
Issued also in French under title: La girafe.
Includes index.
ISBN 0-7172-2488-0

1. Giraffes—Juvenile literature.   I. Title.   II. Series.

QL737.U56S93 1988   j599.73'57   C88-094680-6

Contents

If you were an emperor living a few centuries ago and wanted to make friends with another emperor, what might you offer him as a gift? Gold? Rubies or diamonds? Fine silks? But most emperors already have those things. You want something even more rare and precious, something that will absolutely overwhelm that other emperor. How about a giraffe?

A giraffe! Yes, that is precisely what the Emperor of China chose some 500 years ago when he wanted a gift that would really impress the Emperor of India.

What is so special about a giraffe that it would be considered a gift for kings? Let's take a closer look at this gentle giant of the African plains and find out.

First Steps

Believe it or not, within a few minutes of its birth, a baby giraffe is struggling to its feet. It probably won't make it on the first try—after all it is no simple task to disentangle those long, spindly legs and figure out how to balance that long neck. But with some encouraging nudges and licks from its mother, the youngster will soon sort itself out and be reaching for its first drink of her rich, warm milk.

The young giraffe grows quickly. Within a few weeks it is ready to run and play and keep up with mom and the herd as they move across the plains in search of food. It has a lot to learn, but there will be time for fun too—for a quick romp or a short game of tag.

Keeping close to mom.

Giraffe Country

Scientists tell us that giraffe ancestors used to live in many parts of Africa, Asia and Europe. But that was millions of years ago. Today giraffes and their one living relative, the okapi, are found only in Africa.

The small, shy okapi makes its home in the dense forests of central Africa. Giraffes, on the other hand, live in open woodlands and on the tree-dotted savannas, or plains, where they can move about freely.

Opposite page: *Given their great size, it is easy to understand why giraffes prefer wide open spaces to heavily wooded areas.*

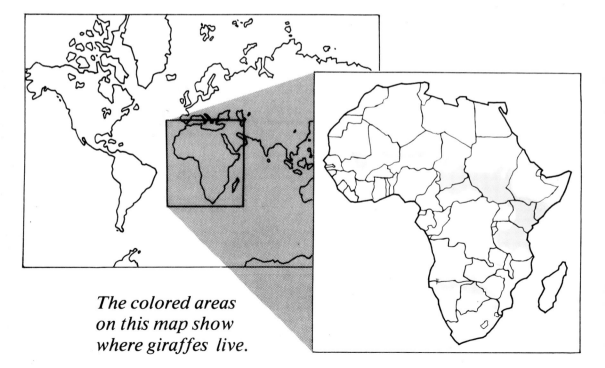

The colored areas on this map show where giraffes live.

Tall, Taller, Tallest

Although the elephant is considered the largest living land mammal because of its tremendous weight, the giraffe is certainly the tallest.

Male giraffes have been known to reach heights of close to six metres (20 feet). That is taller than many two-storey houses! An average male, while not quite that tall, is still huge, and the dainty female, who is shorter yet, often tops 4.5 metres (15 feet).

Even a newborn giraffe may measure in at two metres (over 6 feet), which is taller than most adult men and women.

Because its front legs are longer than its hind legs, the giraffe's body makes one continuous slope from its horns to its tail.

"Going Up!"

What is the first thing you notice about a giraffe? Its l-o-o-o-ng neck, of course. Why would any animal need such a neck?

The giraffe shares its home with huge herds of other plant-eating animals, including zebras, rhinos, elephants and many kinds of antelope. Most of these animals feed on grasses and shrubs. Competition for food could get serious if these low-lying plants had to support giraffes as well. But the giraffe feeds mainly on the leaves and twigs of trees. With its super long neck and legs, it can reach even the top branches.

You may be surprised to hear that a giraffe's neck has only seven bones—exactly the same number as yours. These seven neck bones, or vertebrae as they are called, are simply much, much larger than yours—or any other animal's for that matter! The vertebrae also fit together with special "ball and socket" joints, allowing the giraffe to move its neck smoothly and gracefully.

"How's the weather down there?"

Multipurpose Necks

Giraffes are affectionate creatures and they like to hug each other—just as we do. Of course they do not have arms, so they "hug" by rubbing heads and necks. This is called "necking." It is usually done gently, but sometimes two male giraffes will get a little rough with each other—especially if they are interested in the same female.

Necking then becomes a show of strength, with the males swinging their heads and long necks like wrecking balls. A giraffe's head is quite light for its size, but a male who has had many head-butting battles grows extra layers of bone on his skull. Because of this his head may weigh up to 45 kilograms (100 pounds).

The battle between two males can become quite spectacular. Usually one giraffe—or both—tires after 15 or 20 minutes, and the encounter ends without any serious injury.

Neck to neck.

Overleaf:
Giraffes often serve as walking watchtowers for other animals.

On the Lookout

Thanks to its great height and its remarkable eyesight, the giraffe has an excellent view of its surroundings. Not only can it see over the top of many grassland trees, but the design and location of its eyes give it almost "wrap-around" vision. It can therefore see danger approaching from any direction with only a slight turn of its head.

Giraffes also have acute hearing and a keen sense of smell. No wonder zebras, antelopes and other animals often gather around them to take advantage of their superior lookout skills.

When watching for danger, two heads are better than one.

Getting Around

If you think it would be fun to take a giraffe for a walk, think again. Since a *walking* giraffe covers well over four metres (about 15 feet) with each stride, you would have to run all the way at top speed to keep up.

Giraffes have a very unusual way of walking. They swing both legs on one side of their body at the same time—both right legs, front and hind, then both left legs, front and hind. This way of walking is called *pacing*.

Walking is very definitely the giraffe's preferred way of getting around, but if danger threatens it can gallop at a speed of 50 kilometres (30 miles) an hour, swinging its back feet out together so that they land ahead of its front feet. Because of its size and weight, however, a giraffe cannot keep up this pace for long. As soon as it is out of danger, it slows down to a walk again.

On the move.

Watch that Kick!

Giraffes are peaceable creatures. They don't bother other animals and would rather run from danger than fight. But fight they can and will if attacked or provoked.

Actually, very few animals are foolish enough to attack an adult giraffe. Babies are a different matter, but a giraffe mother will fight fiercely to defend her young. Her powerful legs and dinner-plate-size hoofs are suddenly transformed into deadly sledgehammers, and a single well-aimed kick can kill a full-grown lion.

This comparison of hoof-prints will give you an idea of the size of a giraffe's hoof.

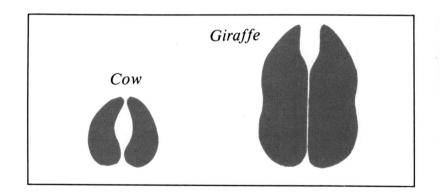

Cow

Giraffe

Only a desperately hungry lion or several acting together will attack anything as big as a full-grown giraffe.

Giraffe Talk

Giraffes are quiet by nature. Because they seldom make sounds, many people believe that they cannot. This is not true. Giraffes may bleat like sheep and snort or moan or moo like cows. They seem to reserve these sounds for extra special occasions, however, such as saying hello to a strange giraffe or greeting a possible mate.

Sounds are not a giraffe's only means of communication. Like many other animals, it also uses body language to let other giraffes know how it is feeling. An angry giraffe, for instance, lowers its head and neck straight out in line with the ground. And to end a fight with another giraffe, the loser will stretch its neck and point its nose skyward. This says, ''I know you are boss!''

One of the giraffe's most obvious message-movements is running. This signals danger to other members of the herd and they will all follow immediately. One gallop says it all.

Sounding off.

25

Horns A-plenty

A giraffe has at least two horns on its head but some bulls, as the males are called, have even more—occasionally as many as five. These horns are an outgrowth of the skull, but unlike those you find on sheep or cattle, they are covered with skin and stiff hairs.

The giraffe is one of the few animals that is born with horns. At first, however, they are made up of softer, gristly material called cartilage. This gradually changes to real bone and becomes very hard as the giraffe gets older.

Although female giraffes, or cows, have horns too, only the males seem to put them to much use. In fact, one quick way to tell a male from a female is to look at their horns. The males usually wear the hair off the ends of theirs by using them when they battle each other to see who's stronger.

The Inside Story

If a giraffe's blood circulation system were just like yours, the poor thing would faint every time it lifted its head up from drinking. Fortunately, the giraffe's circulation system is specially designed for its unusually large size.

First of all, the giraffe needs a very strong heart and plenty of pressure to move the blood from its body all the way up that long neck to its head. With a heart weighing over 12 kilograms (25 pounds) and blood pressure twice that of a human, the giraffe's circulation system is perfectly suited to making sure blood reaches all parts of its body. Also, its veins and arteries are equipped with special trap doors to keep the blood from moving too quickly when the giraffe changes position.

A tree stump makes a handy scratching post for those hard-to-reach places.

Up to one metre (3 feet) long, the tassel of coarse black hair on the end of the giraffe's tail is useful for swishing away flies and other insects.

Personal Patterns

Did you know that giraffes from different places come in different patterns? It's true. Scientists divide giraffes into nine groups based on what part of Africa they live in, their size and color patterns. Even they have trouble telling some of the groups apart, however.

The most easily recognized giraffe is called the Reticulated Giraffe after its pattern of sharply outlined dark patches. The word *reticulated* means "like a net," and that is exactly what the neat, narrow white lines of this giraffe's pattern look like.

The other eight groups of giraffes all come in some variation of a pattern type called *blotched*. Blotched patterns are much less clear and regular than the reticulated pattern.

Belonging to one particular group of giraffes does not mean that you look just like every other giraffe of that group. In fact, every giraffe has its very own arrangement of patches. Just as no one anywhere has fingerprints exactly like yours, no giraffe has spots that exactly match those of any other giraffe.

Tongue Twister

Just think how much ice cream you could get in one lick if you had a tongue as long as your arm! But where would you keep such a tongue when it wasn't in use? Fortunately, the giraffe—which does have a tongue about as long as your arm—has plenty of room for it inside its large head.

The giraffe's remarkable tongue is about 45 centimetres (18 inches) long, narrow, and blackish at the end. It is also very rough and muscular, and the giraffe can use it almost as delicately as you can use your hand. With its tongue, a giraffe can carefully pluck the leaves off even the thorniest tree or twist twigs over its sharp lower teeth to cut them off a branch.

Giraffes have 32 teeth, just like people. But there is one big difference—they have no top front teeth. Instead, they have a bony ridge up front and plenty of broad grinding teeth at the back which they use to chew up their food.

Who needs a knife and fork!

Bring on the Browse

As you may have guessed, giraffes eat a lot. They have to in order to keep their large bodies strong and healthy.

Giraffes are browsers, which means that they feed on twigs and leaves but do not usually eat grass. They spend many hours a day feeding. Bulls often eat 30 kilograms (66 pounds) of food a day and may eat even more. Acacia leaves are a giraffe's favorite food, but they also enjoy mimosa and wild apricot leaves.

Giraffes do not spend a lot of time drinking, and it is just as well they don't. Getting their heads down to water level is an awkward undertaking. It can also be a dangerous one as predators often wait at water holes to attack. Giraffes get most of the water they need from the leaves they eat, but when they do stop for a drink they may take in as much as 35 litres (9 gallons) of water at one time.

Being tall has its advantages—the giraffe can feed on leaves no other animal can reach.

Chew and Chew Again

The giraffe has a specially designed four-part stomach that allows it to get the most from the leaves and twigs that it eats. One part of its stomach also acts as a holding chamber.

A giraffe can eat its meal very quickly because it does not have to bother to chew much before it swallows. Later, when it is relaxing in a safe place, it brings the food back into its mouth to chew it thoroughly. What the giraffe brings back into its mouth is called cud. Other animals, such as deer, cows and camels, also chew their cud.

To avoid the heat of the midday sun, giraffes feed mainly in the early morning and evening.

Traveling Together

The giraffe weighs between 550 and 1800 kilograms (1200–4000 pounds). It takes a LOT of food to keep a body like that running efficiently. To find enough food the giraffe moves over great distances and has no fixed home.

Giraffes usually travel together in herds of 20 to 30 cows and calves. Most bulls travel alone and only join the herd for short periods of time for mating. If there is plenty of food in an area, a herd of 70 or more animals may gather.

Often, with small groups, there is a bull who seems to consider himself a kind of boss. The other giraffes are not too concerned with this, however, and are free to come and go as they like.

Giraffes do most of their traveling and feeding in the morning and evening when it is cool. They rest at night and during the hottest part of the day. A giraffe usually just dozes standing up, but it will occasionally lie down for a short nap, twisting its neck around to rest its head on its back.

What a Baby!

Giraffes can breed all year, although in some areas they do so only between July and September. If there is a herd bull, he will usually father the young, but a male from outside the herd often joins for this purpose. A battle may result, and this is important as it ensures that only the strongest males father the babies.

Fourteen months after breeding, the female gives birth to a single baby weighing 45–70 kilograms (100–150 pounds). The mother stands up while giving birth. This means that the calf has a long drop into this world. But baby giraffes are sturdy creatures. They have to be. Less than an hour after birth they are standing up nursing from their mother.

Feeding on mother's milk.

Giraffe Daycare

The baby giraffe stays alone with its mother for a time, and she does not allow it to mix with other giraffes very often. After a few weeks, however, she joins other cows to share the job of bringing up the babies.

The calves are collected together into a "nursery" where they stay quietly in the shade of trees. They are not allowed to go out into the open plain to feed. The cows take turns, one or two at a time, watching the calves while the other mothers are away feeding. The babysitters are very alert and are always on the watch for danger. Young giraffes are tempting to lions, hyenas and leopards.

The cows return several times during the day to nurse their babies and stay with them throughout the night.

Discovering the great wide world.

Saving Energy

Giraffe babies do play and run, but not nearly as often as other young animals. Instead they spend most of their early months lying peacefully in the shade watching the world around them.

This is important for two reasons. One is that giraffe calves need to protect themselves from losing water to the hot African sun. The other is that they need to save energy for the important task of growing up.

Since even lions are wary of tangling with a full-grown giraffe, growing up is the best protection from hungry hunters. And giraffes grow more quickly than any other mammal baby except the Blue Whale. They may grow over two centimetres (an inch) a day during their first week or two of life, and they almost double their height in the first year.

By the time it is 18 months old,
this calf may be almost as tall as
its mother.

Growing Up

The baby giraffe begins to nibble on leaves and twigs when it is two or three weeks old. It will need its mother's milk for many more months to come, but it must learn what to eat and how to eat it. The giraffe's tongue may be a very good tool for getting hold of plants and twigs, but it takes plenty of practice to make it work properly.

Under the watchful eyes of the adults the calf is well cared for. In a few months it will be ready to join its mother during her daily trips to feed. It will be completely independent by the time it is two years old and will be ready to be a parent on its own a year or two after that. With a little bit of luck, the young giraffe can look forward to 20 or even 25 years of roaming the vast African plains.

Words to Know

Breed To produce young.

Browse Young twigs, leaves and shoots of plants that animals feed on. Also to feed on these things.

Bull Male giraffe.

Calf Baby giraffe.

Cartilage In a young animal, firm rubbery tissue that gradually hardens into bone.

Cow Female giraffe.

Cud Hastily swallowed food brought back to the mouth for chewing by certain animals including deer, cattle and giraffes.

Horns Outgrowths, usually permanent, from the heads of certain animals. In most animals, horns are covered with a hard smooth material, but in the case of the giraffe, they are covered with skin and hair.

Necking Behavior of giraffes that consists of intertwining necks. Most often seen when two males are engaging in a test of strength.

Pacing A way of walking in which both legs on one side of the body are moved at the same time.

Reticulated Word meaning "like a net." Used to describe the pattern of one particular type of giraffe's coat.

Savanna Flat grassland of tropical or subtropical regions.

Vertebrae The individual bones that make up the spinal column.

INDEX

Cover Photo: Tony Stone Worldwide (Masterfile)

Photo Credits: Bill Ivy, pages 4, 13, 24; Harvey Medland (Network Stock Photo File), pages 7, 16-17; The Globe and Mail, Toronto, page 8; FPG International (Masterfile), page 10; Freeman Patterson (Masterfile), pages 14, 39; Zefa (Masterfile), pages 19, 20; Len Pizzen, page 23; Tony Stone Worldwide (Masterfile), pages 27, 40; M. Mara (Valan Photos), page 28; George Calef (Masterfile), page 31; Metro Toronto Zoo, page 32; New York Zoological Society, pages 35, 36; Ron Watts (First Light), pages 43, 44.